Chasing After The Wind

POETRY BY VALERIE J. MACON

Acknowledgements

Shelf Life 2011: "Workshop"
Sleeping Rough 2013: "Morning News"
A String of Black Pearls 2015: "After Valentines Day" and "Harvest"
The Shape of Today 2018: Estate Sale Just Picked Today
Voice and Vision 2020: "1925 Mack"
Page Turner 2021: "What the Squatter Left"
and "Garden Run Amuck"

Then I considered all which my hands had done and labored to do, and behold, all was vanity and chasing after the wind and there was no profit (nothing of lasting value) under the sun.
Ecclesiastes 2:11

THOSE THINGS WE BUILD ON EARTH STAND ONLY
AS TEMPORARY MONUMENTS TO OUR EXISTENCE.
NO MATTER HOW HARD WE TRY, OVER TIME,
THEY SUCCUMB TO THE ELEMENTS
AND THE PASSAGE OF TIME, DEFYING OUR
EFFORTS TO RESIST.
THE UNDENIABLE TRUTH REMAINS, THEY ARE
EVENTUALLY RECLAIMED.

CONTENTS

Who Can Catch the Wind 6
Abandoned and Retaken by the Desert 7
Repossessed Nursing Home 8
Garden Run Amuck 9
This Season's Winner 10
Bully 11
Cabbage after the Freeze 12
Arenal Eruption 13
On Top of a Hurricane 14
Crash 15
Morning News 16
Spider Act 17
Empty Nesters 18
Yesterday 19
1925 Mack Truck 20
Better Times 21
After Valentine's Day 22
Harvest 23
Snap 24
Santa is a Pancake 25
What the Squatter Left 26
Restless Rooms 27
Rebirth of Junk 28
Estate Sale, Just Picked Today 29
Passing On 30
Workshop 31
Alaska's Rushing River 32

Dedication

To Jesse
For His Patient Indulgence

Who Can Catch the Wind

when it sifts through our fingers
like the sands of time,
or trembles through trees
chattering leaves
or waves through meadows
and green grazing fields,

when it gales the seas, lashing ships,
whooshes waters over land
drowning our dwellings,
or batters sand and snow into drifts
that bury our towns,

when it whips wildfires
into consuming blazes
that kindle our treasures,
or blasts our buildings with mighty blows,

Who can catch the wind?
Noone can, when it flies like a bird
unfettered and free,
       it forever will be.

Abandoned and Retaken by the Desert
(Kolmanskop, Nambia)

After the town's people silent fled,
nature's power boldly reached.

Chased by winds, a quiet tide of
rolling sand breached broken windows,
swelling empty halls and vacant rooms,
leaving kitchen tables entombed.
Bathroom tubs were filled
then buried deep in silty hills.

In wind-whipped dunes, bedroom doors
stand ripped and still,
a testament to nature's will.

Repossessed Nursing Home

An army of saplings surrounds,
stilt grass breeches its doorways,
Virginia Creeper crawls through windows,
inches up practical beige walls
now off-colored by graffiti.

Courtyards where the sickly
would sun, once trimmed
in silver-tipped evergreens
and scarlet azaleas, now drown
in groundswell of hairy joint grass.

Gone are those days
when patients languished
waiting for Wednesdays
when church-folk would come
and *Jesus Loves Me* would sing
through the rooftop,
now thatched with vines.

Warty oaks hunch the building,
bust limbs through walls,
roots heave up foundation,
repossessing the land.

Garden Run Amuck

Chaos started among tidy loaves
of house-hugging evergreens,
a bed of red zinnias,
a stand of blue-eyed daisies,
a gleaming gazing ball,

when vines made a slow creep to a tangle
of bush and scattered yard menagerie—
wind spinners, gnomes, toads bearing lanterns,
kissing Dutch figures, whirligig flamingos.

The whine of lawn widgets scared the birds
so they flew far from the snarl of juniper
and top-heavy crepe myrtle hiding
a host of feeders lost in the jumble.

This Season's Winner

There's a gentleman's agreement
between the elements and vegetation:
soil, a nourishing bed from which to spring,
sky, puffs of liquid light,
all poured out in equal measure
on good and evil, just and unjust.

But today the earth thirsts.
Grass withers crisp and brown,
flowers bow their buds and shrivel,
tomatoes languish stunted green on vines.

Yet wily weeds push up through sidewalk cracks,
stretch their homely tendrils across driveways,
lift patio slabs from their union with earth.

Let's give it up for the pluck
of the common weed,
the ultimate survivalist.

Bully

A bully storms into town pitching icy stones,

clatters rooftops, dazes daffodils,
causes tender spring lawns to shiver,

dimples a Prius with a drum roll,
plays disco groove on a Dodge,

slashes dogwoods to ribbons
carpeting yards with wounded leaf litter,

topples pines before blowing out
to bluster the next town over.

Cabbage after the Freeze

The Chinese cabbage, zapped
by last night's artic blast
then stunned into quick thaw
by high noon sun,
has been rendered into gruesome rows
like human brains (bodies buried below).
When squeezed, their rubbery tissue caves,
unfit for harvest.

I flee,
  leaving the garden gate ajar
                    for the rabbits.

Arenal Eruption
(Cost Rica 1968)

Fountains of magma
belch rivers of lava glowing
over lush green-velvet forest

scorching tender orchids,
torching ginger,
banana and cacao.

Throughout the canopy
howler monkeys roar,
sloths startle from slumber.

People of three villages
scramble ahead of the flow,
homes left ashed as Sodom.

Now, like an old man puffing his pipe,
you blow lazy smoke rings
into the blue air over La Fortuna,

sated for a season.
But the dragon in your belly
still fumes.

On Top of a Hurricane

Wedged into slim seats we ascend
above brutish winds, battering rain,
waters breaching their bounds,
climb above felled trees, ripped houses,
cars rushing down street rivers.

We shoot like a silver bullet
through roiling clouds into sky's vault;
seven levels of heaven stacked above,
unfathomed depths of frothy ocean below
black as the bottomless pit.

On each wingtip, a white ray blinks like a dying star.
Even the pilot cannot see through this miasma.
He disengages the throttle of logic
and surrenders our way to a plane-piloting robot.

Crash

In the night sky above Jackson Mississippi
a Piper single-engine plane sputters, whirls,
sprays through blackness like a meteor shower,
spirals until it thunders its nose into the roof
at 10 Willow Street just above the silent
kitchen, apple pie on countertop.

It rips the still like a million doors slammed,
appliances leap off walls, china explodes
from cabinets, silverware spin like boomerangs.
A ball of fire races across the living room,
down hallways, reaches into bedrooms,
shakes sleepers from their feather-down quilts
and out shattered windows.

Morning News

*A family displaced after fire broke out
in their Horsetooth Holler home overnight*
a reporter chants.

In video clip, neighbors plucked
from dreams stand in bunches, mumble
into microphones how they'll pull together
for this decent family, see them through.

But flames already licked
the mouse-and-cheese platter
fresh from yesterday's flee market;
bread and butter pickles,
tomatoes and jams put up
labeled and lined in the pantry;
the finished cross quilt, colors
like the fall garden out back;
photos of Zack on his first day of school
and Ben in his lucky fishing hat
stuck on the refrigerator;
the Lego tower waiting its next story;
the miniature rose in the yard
that struggled to continue
after the first hard frost.

No immediate word on what caused the blaze.

Spider Act

With the grace of a trapeze artist
it springs, swings silky ropes from
Japanese maple to camellia, back flips
and half twists with exquisite form,
interlaces silver threads; then famished,
hangs upside down by his toes, waits.

At halftime, a human stumbles face first
into this astonishing web of spider silk,
shrieks like a carpet clown, plucks
at his clothes, whacks the web witless.

Sure it's a shame, sure it's a lot of work,
but safety net destroyed,
                      the tiny acrobat spins again.

Empty Nesters

Outside my kitchen window
in a Gold Dust bush,
tucked deep in speckled leaf
a robin labors weaving
pine straw threads and sturdy twig,
and there she nestles bright-blue eggs.

For days I watch, until at last
the hatchlings tap their shells
emerging blind and naked,
helpless and hungry
under parents watchful eye.
Back and forth they scrub,
digging worm and grub to feed
their brood of chirping chicks.

In sultry summer-morning haze,
a cawing crow circles slow, then,
swoops and snatches swift and sly,
with greedy beak claims its prize.
Again it strikes, and then again
until the parents' sad return—

empty nesters.

Yesterday

Each new morning
as coffee drizzles into cups,
the secondhand on the wall clock
ticks around its face
adding and subtracting time.

In the shadows,
a reaper swings his sickle,
harvesting minutes.

The Earth spins on its axis
one-thousand miles per hour.
The sun darts across the heavens
until the moon spins into place.

And today becomes yesterday.

1925 Mack Truck

Back in its day, it was a workhorse,
a powerhouse of raw truck.
Year after year its cylinders pushed
through a hard day's labor
till one by one its parts wore out.

Now, sidelined under an oak,
branches twist a coffin over its shell.
Vines weave webs through its bones,
leaves press against panes, weeds
poke through rusted floorboard.
Its fine wooden doors, beetles' meal.

The earth continues to overpower the feeble,
claim us back, break us down to our elements
—calcium, carbon, nitrogen, phosphorous—
recycling and repurposing us.

With each passing year our proud stories
decay, our existence becomes more elusive,
slipping into the realm of dinosaur bones.

Better Times

Out front Bob and Jack Filling Station
tangled in pigweed
a Coca Cola sign still reads
Gas War 50 Cent. In better times,

a pump jockey, rag spilling out back pocket,
would smile, fill tanks, check dipsticks,
rake his long-handled sponge
over windshields, top tires with air.

Today, like a worried mother,
a lone pump stands watch—
round-faced, hose and nozzle
posed on its rusty hip.

Across the street, bulldozers
strip the land down to raw red dirt.
Felled pines are rolled off
in flatbeds to the hereafter,
backhoes buck the earth aside

to make way for a blazing new Sheets.

After Valentine's Day

On a polished walnut vanity
a dozen roses stand on firm long stems,
bunched in pear-shaped crystal
adorned in glossy foliage,
cheeks flushed fresh pink,
perfume sweeter than
dark chocolate truffles.

It seems like only days pass—
huddled in Waterford Irish Lace
they slump over canes,
bow their wizened heads,
form dowager's humps.
Additives depleted, their water
turns foam and sour milk.

Harvest

A lifetime of tillage cultivated
the old farmer's back into a hump,
plowed him down at the hips,
bent him horizontal as an ox,
fixed his eyes on the earth,
now a field of street minutia—
crushed coffee cup, flicked cigarette butt,
crinkled Almond Joy wrapper,
Superman figure without a head—
and he rattles his cane to Beefy's
where a crop of hoary heads gather
at noon around the checkerboard.

Snap

Poplar, pine, or sturdy oak,
they all have one thing in common:
during calm summer days,
seemingly healthy tree limbs
simply snap and fall off.

The aged, even those who seem healthy,
are prone to fall, snapping bones:
arms, legs, knees, hips, and ribs,
splintering wrists and ankles.
They go dormant for months,
fading from the chitchat of neighbors
and their prayers.

Then, after retiring the college debt
of their young doctor, they reappear
pinned, stitched and snapped together
with metal plates and screws.

Santa is a Pancake

draped over the front pitch
of the roof, beside the chimney,
all his jolly and hot air deflated;
his suit, once red and merry,
now a sullied pool of plastic
collecting rain and soot in its creases.

One could only imagine
a carload of teens full of hormones
popping him with a riddle of rocks;
or, the nick of a woodpecker
starting a slow leak;
or, Santa himself trying to squeeze down
the too-tight chimney causing a blowout.

And this, a few weeks before Christmas
when he should be standing tall
on the rooftop, finger beside nose,
sack slung over back.

To make matters worse, just down the block,
his eight tiny reindeer also lay dashed.

What the Squatter Left

In Old San Juan, where cobbled streets
are lined with homes of cheerful
orange, green and breezy blues,
an abandoned house on Calle Luna
stands apart, a haunted shell of faded grays.

Behind its murky windows in empty rooms
of moldy walls and musty air,
the traces of a squatter's life remain:

a toothbrush and a twisted tube of paste,
a mattress stained and stale,
some needles scattered on the squalid floor,
and sketched across a peeling wall,
crude and vulgar art— a naked woman
with a pair of eyes where breasts should be,
a mockery of the heart.
.

Restless Rooms

Their scheme cannot be grasped or held.
  Stacked-book cocktail table runs off
to serve a Queen Anne couch,
  curvy-legged ottoman fills its void,
Ficus on a plant stand swaps
  with two upholstered chairs, Asian
lamp that yesterday cast its pool of light
  between sunroom chairs now
takes a living room corner,
  bookcase goes AWOL from fireplace nook,
walnut end-table snatches its place.
  Art jumps walls—Red Bowl print
bounces sunroom, hall, kitchen,
  pauses to rest beside a front room window.
Accent pillows plump and shuffle,
  flip-flop couch to chair.
Even a garbage can, long hidden in
  a laundry closet, has now come out
to take an open stance beside the refrigerator.

Rebirth of Junk

The sought after, coveted,
craved for, and needed:
bicycles, barbeques, playsets
and printers, silver and crystal,
bone china, and wind spinners—
now a castaway list,
a symphony of treasures
turned into clutter.

Got Junk? The roadside sign asks.
A prompt to release. They'll come
when I call, whisk my burdens away.
My only part, to point, they say.

Their service comes with a promise—
they'll rebirth my junk to others
who store up *their* hoard of treasures
in vain hope of finding pleasure.

Estate Sale, Just Picked Today

Sermons of spent time
burnished with dust,
room after room of stuff
found heaped and pressed
in someone's left-behind house.

The had-to-haves
paid for with sweat and soul.
The fruit of overtime,
lost weekends, and children
adrift. Grandma's highboy,
and the silver of family feuds.

A woman picks through a pile of vinyls:
Elvis, Beatles, Beach Boys, Chipmunks.
She calls out to her young son,
When I say 'record' this is what I mean.
The boy, plugged with earbuds, nods.

Passing On

Estate sales make me want to purge,
whittle down glut, remove surplus of silly
nick knacks, armies of crystal, tarnished
silver, and grandma's ornate dinnerware.

Today shoppers rummage, roll their eyes
through musty rooms of orphaned excess:
twenty pairs of white jeans,
thirty keepsake Santas,
a dusty horde of porcelain figurines.

The living carry home couches, curios,
vases and vanities for their own
inevitable estate sale.

Workshop

Coffee cans
lined up
like tin soldiers
rusty kick
of nuts, bolts
paintbrush stiff
with shellac
hot tang
of soldering iron
fresh sawdust
oily zest
of lawnmower
ripe breath
of Miracle-Gro
and half-empty sacks
of rye seed
scarred workbench
hammers
worn smooth
screwdriver armies
perplexed
in a maze of hooks
and on a wooden peg
a plaid flannel shirt,
stained with the sweet
savor of your handiwork.

Alaska's Rushing River

A Greek philosopher once said
the only thing constant is change.
But I say, consider the constant
Nenana River.

For centuries now she has chuckled
cold and swift over rock and limb,
sluicing though mountains that rise
like jagged paper cutouts from her shores,

past ancient black spruce, quaking aspen,
birch and wild blueberry.
She carries lamprey and lake chubs,
silver salmon and slimy sculpins in her flow.

She wooshes rafters through her rapids
in a wild tilt and spin ride,
and though many a beaver has
stacked trunk and branch in her tide,

she snickers over logjams with
a riot of whitecaps and rushes on.
Trying to stop her is like
      . . . chasing after the wind.

www.ingramcontent.com/pod-product-compliance
Lightning Source LLC
Chambersburg PA
CBHW050450010526
44118CB00013B/1769